War Planes

Heavy Bombers:
The B-52 Stratofortresses

by Michael and Gladys Green

CAPSTONE
HIGH-INTEREST
BOOKS

an imprint of Capstone Press
Mankato, Minnesota

Capstone High-Interest Books are published by Capstone Press
151 Good Counsel Drive, P.O. Box 669, Mankato, Minnesota 56002
http://www.capstone-press.com

Library of Congress Cataloging-in-Publication Data
Green, Michael, 1952–
    Heavy bombers: the B-52 Stratofortresses /by Michael and Gladys Green.
    p. cm.—(War planes)
    Summary: Describes the history, weapons, equipment, and use by the Air Force of
the B-52 bomber, nicknamed the "Big Ugly Fat Fellow" (BUFF) by flight crews because
of its size and appearance.
    Includes bibliographical references and index.
    ISBN 0-7368-2151-1 (hardcover)
    1. B-52 bomber—Juvenile literature. [1. B-52 bomber. 2. Bombers.] I. Green,
Gladys, 1954– II. Title. III. Series.
UG1242.B6G7197 2004
623.7'463—dc21   2003000056

Editorial Credits
Christine Peterson, editor; Timothy Halldin, series designer; Patrick Dentinger, book
    designer; Jo Miller, photo researcher; Eric Kudalis product planning editor

Photo Credits
Corbis/George Hall, 9; Boyd Belcher, 23
Defense Visual Information Center (DVIC), cover, 1, 4, 10, 18, 20, 24, 26
Photri-Microstock, 7
Ted Carlson/Fotodynamics, 13, 16–17, 29

Consultant
Raymond L. Puffer, Ph.D, Historian, Air Force Flight Test Center, Edwards Air Force
Base, California

1 2 3 4 5 6 08 07 06 05 04 03

Table of Contents

The B-52 in Action

Two groups of U.S. Air Force B-52 bombers fly toward a terrorist training base in an enemy country. The huge gray planes carry dozens of heavy bombs under their wings. More weapons fill storage areas inside the B-52s.

The B-52 crews know they have a dangerous job. Enemy soldiers at missile sites in the area could attack their planes. The first group of B-52 planes will attack enemy missile sites on the ground.

The first group of B-52s attacks the ground targets before the second group of B-52s arrives. The B-52 crews fire missiles when they are more than 1,000 miles (1,600 kilometers) away. The weapons strike missile sites guarding the terrorist base.

The second group of B-52s arrives at the training base. The U.S. planes drop their bombs over the enemy base. The powerful explosions destroy the terrorist camp. B-52 pilots see more than 100 large, deep holes made by the bombs. Once again, the B-52s and their crews have defended their country.

The B-52 is the largest bomber used by the Air Force.

About the B-52

Since 1955, the B-52 Stratofortress has been the Air Force's main heavy bomber. Flight crews call the B-52 "Big Ugly Fat Fellow" (BUFF) because of its size. The heavy bomber is more than 159 feet (48 meters) long. The B-52 stretches 185 feet (56 meters) between the tips of its wings.

The U.S. Air Force began making plans for the B-52 after World War II (1939–1945). Air Force officials decided they needed a new plane that would be faster than other bombers.

Early types of bombers used engines that were driven by propellers. These planes were expensive to build. They also were difficult to fix. Air Force officials decided that the new bomber would be powered by jet engines.

The Boeing Military Airplane Company began work on the new bomber in 1946. Pilots took the B-52 for its first test flight in April 1952. The Air Force began using the plane three years later.

Between 1954 and 1962, Boeing built 744 B-52s. Over the years, the Air Force used six different models of the plane. Only 80 B-52H bombers are still in service.

All B-52 models are powered by eight jet engines.

Chapter Two

Learn About

- The B-52's flight crews
- Bomb bay
- B-52 engines

Inside the B-52

The B-52 is a huge plane that can carry several crew members and many different bombs. The B-52's five crew members work on two flight decks. A huge bomb bay stores the plane's weapons.

The B-52's eight jet engines provide enough power for the plane to carry several tons of weapons. The B-52 weighs more than 200 tons (181 metric tons) when loaded with fuel and weapons.

Flight Crew

Each member of the B-52 flight crew has a different job to do on the plane. The pilot and co-pilot control the plane in flight. The radar navigator helps the pilot and co-pilot safely fly over rough ground at low altitudes. The radar navigator also fires the B-52's weapons. The mission navigator guides the plane to and from targets.

The electronic warfare officer (EWO) guards the plane from enemy attack. The EWO uses radar to check for missiles and gunfire that could hit the plane. If enemy missiles are spotted, the EWO fires flares from under the B-52's wings. Missiles then follow the heat from these flares instead of the B-52.

Bomb Bay

The B-52 was made to carry many large bombs and missiles. The B-52 stores its weapons inside a large area under the plane's body called a bomb bay. The number of weapons changes based on their size and weight.

The B-52 has flown bombing missions since 1955.

The bomb bay is more than 28 feet (9 meters) long and 6 feet (2 meters) wide. Three sets of heavy doors cover the bomb bay underneath the plane. Motors open the doors when the bombs are dropped.

Engines

All B-52s use jet engines. With these engines, the bomber can travel greater distances at faster speeds than other bombers.

All models of the B-52 use Pratt & Whitney engines. Each engine produces 17,000 pounds (7,711 kilograms) of thrust. Thrust is the force that pushes a jet plane forward. The engines help the B-52s reach a top speed of 650 miles (1,046 kilometers) per hour.

The B-52H uses eight turbofan jet engines. These newer jet engines are more powerful than the engines on other B-52s.

New Sensors

Since 1971, the Air Force has equipped the B-52 with better sensors to protect the plane from enemy attack. The AN/ASQ-151 Electro-Optical Viewing System (EVS) uses two sensors set

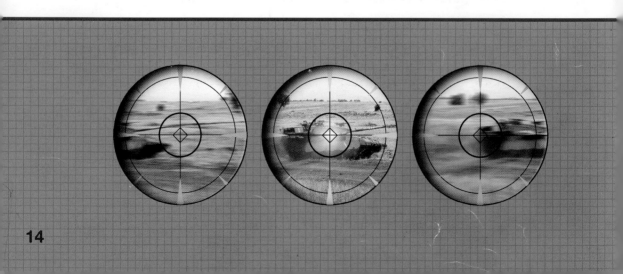

B-52 Specifications

Function:	Heavy bomber
Manufacturer:	Boeing Military Airplane Company
Date Deployed:	1955
Length:	159 feet, 4 inches (49 meters)
Wingspan:	185 feet (56 meters)
Height:	40 feet, 8 inches (12 meters)
Engines:	eight Pratt & Whitney TF33-P3/103 turbofans
Thrust:	17,000 pounds (7,711 kilograms) per engine
Speed:	650 miles (1,046 kilometers) per hour
Ceiling:	50,000 feet (15,240 meters)
Range:	Unlimited with in-flight refueling

in small spinning turrets. One sensor is a low-light-level television (LLL-TV) unit. The LLL-TV uses light from outside the plane to give the pilot a picture of the ground. The B-52 also uses a forward-looking infrared (FLIR) unit. The FLIR turns heat from objects outside the plane into a picture for the pilot.

vertical fin

wing

stabilizer

fuel tank

16

The B-52 Stratofortress

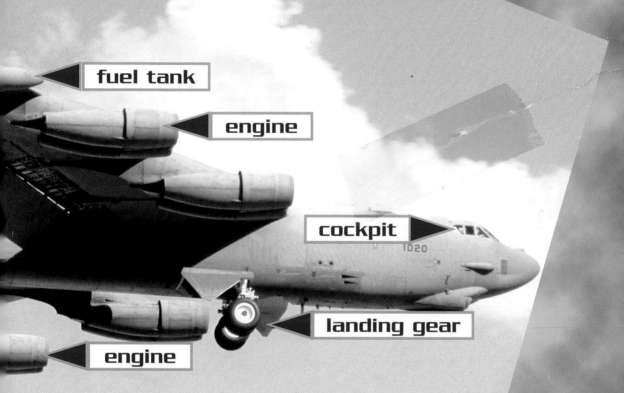

fuel tank

engine

cockpit

1020

landing gear

engine

Chapter Three

Learn About

- Nuclear cruise missiles
- Iron bombs
- Standoff weapons

Weapons and Tactics

B-52s have carried almost every kind of nuclear and non-nuclear weapon used by the Air Force. The B-52 can drop bombs while flying at an altitude of 40,000 feet (12,192 meters).

In 1955, the B-52 carried large nuclear weapons weighing more than 7,000 pounds (3,175 kilograms). The B-52's bomb bay now holds large iron bombs. The B-52 also carries smaller nuclear and non-nuclear bombs and missiles.

The B-52 drops a series of bombs over targets.

Nuclear Bombs

The B53 is the most powerful nuclear bomb carried by the B-52H. The B53 bomb has the same explosive power as 9 million pounds (4 million kilograms) of TNT.

The B53 bomb weighs 8,850 pounds (4,014 kilograms.) The B-52 can carry two B53 bombs in its bay.

The B-52 also can carry smaller nuclear bombs. The B61 bomb has the explosive power of 2 million pounds (907,186 kilograms) of TNT. The B-52H can carry eight of these bombs.

Non-nuclear Bombs

The B-52H also uses non-nuclear or plain bombs. The plane can hold between 12 and 25 plain bombs in its bomb bay. The B-52 can also carry more bombs under its wings. The bombs can weigh between 500 pounds (227 kilograms) and 2,000 pounds (907 kilograms).

The B-52 also has guided bombs on board. The Joint Standoff Weapon (JSOW) uses data from satellites in space to find targets. The JSOW can travel 40 miles (64 kilometers) to its target.

Nuclear Cruise Missiles

Nuclear cruise missiles help B-52s safely reach their targets. These weapons are called "standoff weapons." B-52 crews use these missiles to hit weapons sites on the ground. Once enemy weapons have been destroyed, the B-52s can safely complete their missions.

The B-52 fires two types of cruise missiles. Both missiles use jet engines to reach their targets.

The Air Launched Cruise Missile-86B (ALCM-86B) can travel more than 1,500 miles (2,400 kilometers) to a target. The missile is guided by information from space satellites that circle the Earth. The B-52 can carry six of these missiles.

In 1990, the B-52 added the newer Advanced Cruise Missile, ACM-129A. This

Crews get ready to load training mines on a B-52.

missile can hit targets that are 1,800 miles
(2,897 kilometers) away. The ACM-129A uses
an internal navigation system to locate targets.
The B-52H can carry up to 20 of these missiles.

Bombs can be attached under the B-52's wings.

Standoff Missiles

B-52s also can fire standoff missiles to hit targets that are farther away. In 1986, non-nuclear warheads were placed on some standard cruise missiles. These missiles are air-to-ground, conventional air-launched cruise missiles. These missiles are called AGM-86C CALCM. The AGM–86C uses data from satellites to find targets.

The Air Force is working on a new model of the CALCM. The AGM-86D CALCM will attack targets that are hidden underground.

The AGM-142 Have Nap is a medium-range missile. This missile hits targets up to 45 miles (72 kilometers) away. The Have Nap uses either a TV camera or infrared sensor to find targets.

The B-52H can also fire an AGM-84D Harpoon antiship missile. The Harpoon missile is loaded with a 500-pound (227 kilogram) warhead. It can hit ships more than 100 miles (160 kilometers) away. The B-52H can carry 12 of these missiles under its wings.

Chapter Four

Learn About

- B-52 improvements
- New bombers
- Electronic warfare aircraft

The Future

The B-52 took its first test flight more than 50 years ago. Today, the heavy bomber is still an important part of the Air Force. The B-52 has new equipment and updated parts.

More than 740 B-52s were made between 1954 and 1962. The bombers were located at 38 U.S. Air Force bases around the country. Today, there are fewer than 80 B-52H bombers in service. Of these, only 56 B-52Hs are used in combat. The other planes are used for training.

In 2003, B-52s flew bombing missions for the U.S. Air Force as part of Operation Iraqi Freedom.

Changes for the B-52

The Air Force now uses newer bombers on missions. The B-1B Lancer and B-2 Spirit are now sent on missions at low altitudes. The B-52H only flies close to targets when there are no enemy weapons in the area. The B-52H is mainly used to fire missiles at enemy targets that are far away.

The B-52H uses a safer radio system. Messages sent on the older radios could be picked up or blocked by the enemy. Now, B-52 flight crews use a digital system to send information. Enemy forces cannot block or get data that is sent on the new digital system.

A New Job for the B-52

The Air Force may turn some B-52H bombers into electronic warfare (EW) aircraft. EW planes do not drop bombs on enemy ground positions. Instead, this type

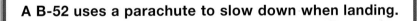

A B-52 uses a parachute to slow down when landing.

of aircraft carries equipment to jam enemy radio and radar systems.

The B-52 has been in service longer than any other war plane. The newest B-52 planes are older than most of their pilots. The B-52 will continue to serve in combat for many more years.

Words to Know

altitude (AL-ti-tood)—the height a plane flies above the ground

exhaust (eg-ZAWST)—heated air leaving a jet engine

propeller (pruh-PEL-ur)—a set of rotating blades that pulls a plane through the air

radar (RAY-dar)—equipment that uses radio waves to locate and guide objects

sensor (SEN-sur)—an instrument that detects physical changes in the environment

TNT (TEE-en-tee)—a flammable compound that is used as an explosive

turbofan engine (TUR-boh-fan EN-juhn)— a jet engine powered by a rotating fan

turret (TUR-it)—a part of an aircraft that holds a gun or sensors; turrets turn so that sensors can pick up light from all directions.

warhead (WOR-hed)—the part of a missile that carries explosives

To Learn More

Chant, Christopher. *Role of the Fighter and Bomber.* The World's Greatest Aircraft. Philadelphia: Chelsea House, 2000.

Holden, Henry M. *Air Force Aircraft.* Aircraft. Berkeley Heights, N.J.: Enslow, 2001.

Maynard, Christopher. *Aircraft.* The Need for Speed. Minneapolis: Lerner, 1999.

Useful Addresses

Air Combat Command
Public Affairs Office
115 Thompson Street, Suite 104
Langley Air Force Base, VA 23665-1987

Air Force Flight Test Center
History Office
305 East Popson Avenue
Edwards Air Force Base, CA 93524-6595

Internet Sites

Do you want to find out more about B-52 Stratofortresses? Let FactHound, our fact-finding hound dog, do the research for you.

Here's how:

1) Visit *http://www.facthound.com*
2) Type in the **Book ID** number: **0736821511**
3) Click on **FETCH IT**.

FactHound will fetch Internet sites picked by our editors just for you!

Index